# BOUNDARIES

## ARE SELF-CARE

A Journal to Help You Set Boundaries,
Redefine Strength, and Put Yourself First

**ASHA GIBSON**

CASTLE POINT BOOKS

NEW YORK

www.castlepointbooks.com

The Castle Point Books trademark is owned by Castle Point Publishing, LLC.
Castle Point books are published and distributed by St. Martin's Publishing Group.

ISBN 978-1-250-28541-6 (trade paperback)

Design by Joanna Price
Edited by Monica Sweeney

Images used under license by Shutterstock.com

Our books may be purchased in bulk for promotional, educational, or business
use. Please contact your local bookseller or the Macmillan Corporate and
Premium Sales Department at 1-800-221-7945, extension 5442, or by email at
MacmillanSpecialMarkets@macmillan.com.

First Edition: 2023

10 9 8 7 6 5 4 3 2 1

First things first: you need and deserve a protective system that you can rely on. Boundaries keep you well and allow you enough space to prevent burnout, exhaustion, and becoming overwhelmed.

What's one boundary that you know you
need to set but you're afraid to?

What's the consequence you're afraid of if you set that boundary?

How would your life improve if that boundary were in place?

....................................................................................................................................................

....................................................................................................................................................

....................................................................................................................................................

....................................................................................................................................................

....................................................................................................................................................

....................................................................................................................................................

....................................................................................................................................................

....................................................................................................................................................

....................................................................................................................................................

....................................................................................................................................................

....................................................................................................................................................

....................................................................................................................................................

....................................................................................................................................................

....................................................................................................................................................

....................................................................................................................................................

....................................................................................................................................................

Be open to

# UNLEARNING.

Most commonly, boundaries are either nonexistent or given a bad name. To begin setting healthy boundaries, you need to be willing to unlearn the unhelpful messages that have guided your relationship with boundaries.

**What messages were you taught about boundaries? What has been your relationship with boundaries?**

..........................................................................................................................................
..........................................................................................................................................
..........................................................................................................................................
..........................................................................................................................................
..........................................................................................................................................
..........................................................................................................................................
..........................................................................................................................................
..........................................................................................................................................
..........................................................................................................................................
..........................................................................................................................................
..........................................................................................................................................
..........................................................................................................................................
..........................................................................................................................................
..........................................................................................................................................
..........................................................................................................................................
..........................................................................................................................................
..........................................................................................................................................

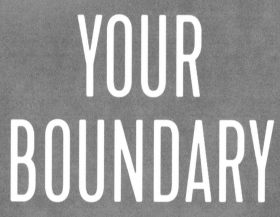

# YOUR BOUNDARY

is a complete
sentence.

You have the right to hold others accountable when they behave in a way that feels harmful to you. You do not need to overexplain or prove the validity of your boundary. Setting a boundary is a valid response and a complete sentence.

**What do you consider to be boundary violations?**
**How do you handle boundary violations?**
**How would you like to handle them?**

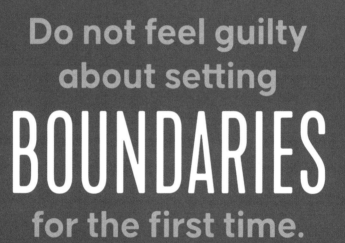

Do not feel guilty about setting

# BOUNDARIES

for the first time.

Boundaries can be proactive and reactive. You may set a boundary
to guide the initial nature of the relationship or you may find yourself
setting a boundary to readjust the course of the relationship.
Either way, be open to releasing the guilt of protecting yourself.

**Do you find yourself setting boundaries proactively or reactively?
What would make you feel less guilty about setting the boundary?**

Strive to be

# PROTECTIVE,

## not perfect.

When setting boundaries, do not strive for perfection. There is no perfect boundary nor is there the perfect way to set a boundary. When centering your protection, focus on what you need instead of making sure it is "right."

**What is one boundary you have been working on setting?**
**How has perfection interfered with you setting it?**

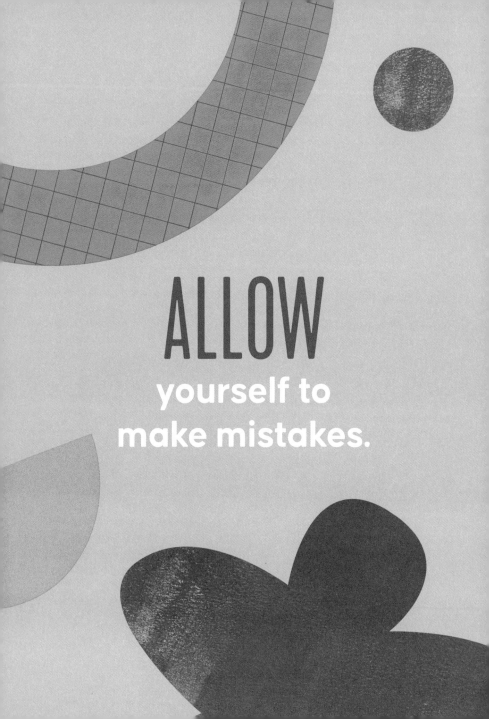

# ALLOW
## yourself to make mistakes.

When setting boundaries for the first time, or setting a new boundary, you may or may not get it right the first, second, or third time—and that is okay. Make room for trial and error; it is a part of the process.

**What's a boundary you set but struggled to maintain?**
**What makes it hard for you to enforce that boundary?**

........................................................................................
........................................................................................
........................................................................................
........................................................................................
........................................................................................
........................................................................................
........................................................................................
........................................................................................
........................................................................................
........................................................................................
........................................................................................
........................................................................................
........................................................................................
........................................................................................
........................................................................................
........................................................................................
........................................................................................

# Take small
# STEPS.

The truth is, setting boundaries can be scary and uncomfortable. Do not try to set every boundary today. Take small steps when beginning to set boundaries or setting a new boundary. This will prevent you from becoming too overwhelmed and withdrawing the boundary.

**What is one boundary you can set today?**
**What are two small steps you can take toward setting this boundary?**

...................................................................................................................

...................................................................................................................

...................................................................................................................

...................................................................................................................

...................................................................................................................

...................................................................................................................

...................................................................................................................

...................................................................................................................

...................................................................................................................

...................................................................................................................

...................................................................................................................

...................................................................................................................

...................................................................................................................

...................................................................................................................

...................................................................................................................

Treat

# YOURSELF

how you want
others to treat you.

Your needs must be met by you first. By meeting your own needs, you will be able to identify what your standards look and feel like, and you won't be swayed into accepting anything less.

**How do you want to be treated?**
**How do you not want to be treated?**

Keep the

# PROMISES

you make
to yourself.

One way to strengthen boundaries within yourself is not to go back on the promise you made yourself. This is also a great way to build trust within yourself and honor your self-worth.

**What is a promise you have made yourself that you've broken? How did it make you feel?**

**What is one thing you can do to make sure you do not break that promise again?**

Say

# YES

to rest.

Ignoring when you need rest violates your own boundaries. It is hard to enjoy the fruits of your labor when you are exhausted once you have reached your goal. Even with your busy schedule, there are opportunities for rest, but you must be intentional about welcoming them.

**What does rest look like for you?**
**How can you incorporate more rest within your daily life?**

...................................................................................................................................................

...................................................................................................................................................

...................................................................................................................................................

...................................................................................................................................................

...................................................................................................................................................

...................................................................................................................................................

...................................................................................................................................................

...................................................................................................................................................

...................................................................................................................................................

...................................................................................................................................................

...................................................................................................................................................

...................................................................................................................................................

...................................................................................................................................................

...................................................................................................................................................

...................................................................................................................................................

...................................................................................................................................................

# LISTEN

to your body;
stop when
it says stop.

———

Pushing yourself beyond your limit is another boundary violation, and there are often consequences that result from pushing yourself too far. Your body will let you know what it needs and when it needs it.

**How often do you push yourself beyond your limit?**
**How can you be more in tune with what your body needs?**

Any time is the right time when it comes to centering your

# WELLNESS.

Do not wait for the "right time" to take care of yourself. Make time for your wellness. Neglecting your wellness prioritizes the potential for illness.

**On a scale of 1–10, how would you rate the way you have been taking care of yourself? Identify two ways you can improve that rating.**

Do not wait until you are sick to pay attention to

# YOUR HEALTH.

You deserve care and attention without being sick. Be it physical, mental, emotional, spiritual, or financial—the state of your overall well-being is dependent upon how much time, attention, and care you give it daily.

**In what areas of your life are you not feeling the best?**
**What are you willing to do to improve your wellness in those areas?**

.................................................................................................................................
.................................................................................................................................
.................................................................................................................................
.................................................................................................................................
.................................................................................................................................
.................................................................................................................................
.................................................................................................................................
.................................................................................................................................
.................................................................................................................................
.................................................................................................................................
.................................................................................................................................
.................................................................................................................................
.................................................................................................................................
.................................................................................................................................
.................................................................................................................................
.................................................................................................................................
.................................................................................................................................
.................................................................................................................................

# SELF-CARE

**should be an everyday effort.**

Make yourself a self-care plan for every day, not just
something to incorporate when you are not feeling well.
By establishing a self-care plan, you will have tangible go-to's
to pull from when you are not feeling your best.

**What do you need to feel good and most like yourself?**

**What are two ways you can incorporate
that into a daily plan for yourself?**

Create space
in your life just for
YOU.

You give so much of yourself to everyone and everything that sometimes it is hard to recognize when you have neglected yourself. Before your day starts, in the middle of your day, and at the end of your day, create time and space that is dedicated just to you.

**How much time have you set aside just for you?**
**What is one thing that you can do today that is just for you?**

....................................................................................................................................................
....................................................................................................................................................
....................................................................................................................................................
....................................................................................................................................................
....................................................................................................................................................
....................................................................................................................................................
....................................................................................................................................................
....................................................................................................................................................
....................................................................................................................................................
....................................................................................................................................................
....................................................................................................................................................
....................................................................................................................................................
....................................................................................................................................................
....................................................................................................................................................
....................................................................................................................................................

Shift your
thinking to more

# HELPFUL

thoughts.

What you think about yourself matters. The thoughts you choose to keep will shape how you will choose to interact in life. For example, instead of thinking "I'm not doing enough," make an effort to shift your thinking to "I'm doing my best."

**What are some unhelpful thoughts that you hold on to?**

**Write down your unhelpful thoughts, scratch them out, and then write down a helpful thought that challenges them.**

# Your

## VOICE

### is the voice you will hear the most.

Speak to yourself with kindness and compassion. Use words that create a healthy internal environment. How you talk to yourself has a significant impact on how you treat yourself and how you view the world.

Identify five positive things about yourself.
How can you use those positive characteristics
to speak better to yourself?

........................................................................................................................................................

........................................................................................................................................................

........................................................................................................................................................

........................................................................................................................................................

........................................................................................................................................................

........................................................................................................................................................

........................................................................................................................................................

........................................................................................................................................................

........................................................................................................................................................

........................................................................................................................................................

........................................................................................................................................................

........................................................................................................................................................

........................................................................................................................................................

........................................................................................................................................................

........................................................................................................................................................

........................................................................................................................................................

Do not use negative words as a source for

# MOTIVATION.

Criticizing yourself will not produce positive change. If anything, critical language will push you back into a cycle of harmful behavior patterns.

**What critical language do you use with yourself when you make a mistake?**
**Identify positive words you can use to replace the critical ones.**

# Choose to
# DISCONNECT.

Disconnect from people, places, and things that no longer
serve you, make you feel good, or make you feel whole.

Identify environments, people, or habits that you once
enjoyed but no longer have a positive effect.

What makes you feel good? What makes you feel whole?
Which people or what environments produce that feeling for you?

# DO NOT
## give up.

It is completely common for boundaries to feel unnatural and uncomfortable when you are setting them for the first time. It is also natural to feel as if the boundary may be wrong when someone challenges it. Although you may experience these emotions, do not give up on discovering the best way to protect yourself.

**What responses cause you to stop setting boundaries?**
**Write down the reminders you would**
**need to push past the discomfort.**

# LIMIT

**your engagement
with anyone who
mismanaged their
access to you.**

It could feel extremely overwhelming for others to have unlimited access to you. Although setting boundaries can be scary and uncomfortable, remember that you do not have to accept behavior that dishonors you.

**What responses from others might cause you to second-guess setting boundaries?**

**How would you feel if you did not set the boundary?**

........................................................................................................................

........................................................................................................................

........................................................................................................................

........................................................................................................................

........................................................................................................................

........................................................................................................................

........................................................................................................................

........................................................................................................................

........................................................................................................................

........................................................................................................................

........................................................................................................................

........................................................................................................................

........................................................................................................................

........................................................................................................................

........................................................................................................................

........................................................................................................................

# Your routine
# MATTERS.

Work days can sometimes be unpredictable. This is why it is important to create your own routine that helps you to stay balanced. If you are unable to create a routine at work, create a routine before reporting to work.

**What are three things that help you feel calm and centered?**

**Write out a routine that includes you engaging in one or all three of those things before or during work.**

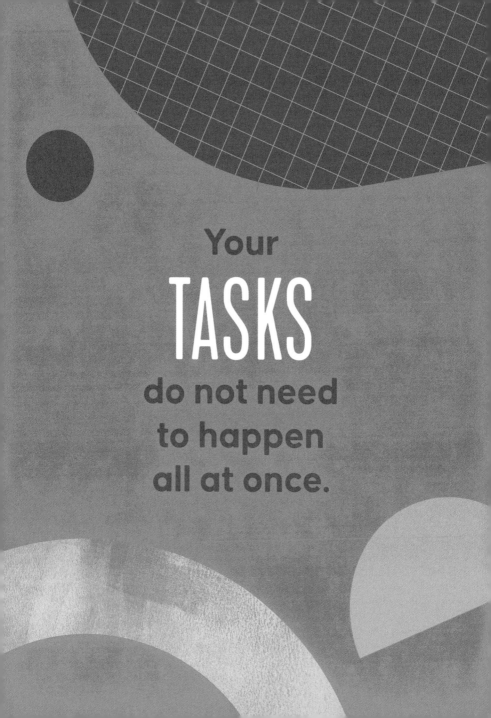

Create healthy boundaries within your work environment.
Arrange your tasks in a way that works for you during
times when you function at your best.

Identify your peak performance times of the day and which
work-related tasks would best fit into those time slots.

If you're working on a project with multiple components, schedule
the components into your workday or workweek ahead of time.

# YOU
**do not have
to do it all alone.**

If the task is too much for you to manage, transfer it. Knowing your limits is one way to honor your boundaries, and it also makes you a more effective employee.

**What stops you from asking for help or transferring the task? Write out a script that helps you communicate why a task needs to be shared, or transferred, and why.**

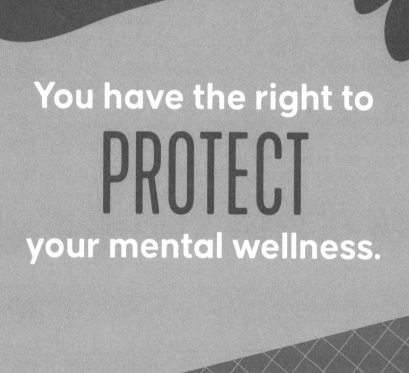

You have the right to

# PROTECT

your mental wellness.

You are the only one that truly knows how your work-related tasks impact you. If you do not have the space to complete someone else's task, you have the right to say no to additional responsibilities.

What stops you from saying no to requests from coworkers? Identify two phrases you can use to comfortably decline a coworker's request to take on additional responsibilities.

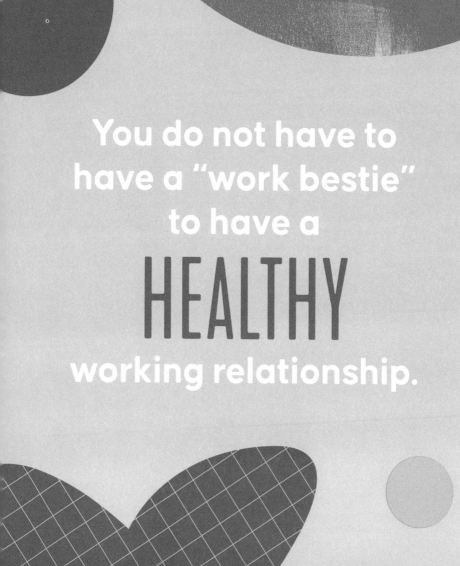

You do not have to have a "work bestie" to have a HEALTHY working relationship.

Separating personal and professional relationships is an effective boundary to set within working environments. You can have healthy professional relationships with your coworkers without telling them intimate details of your life or hanging out with them outside of work hours.

Identify the ways you have allowed professional relationships to become personal.

What are two ways you can make sure that work-related relationships remain professional?

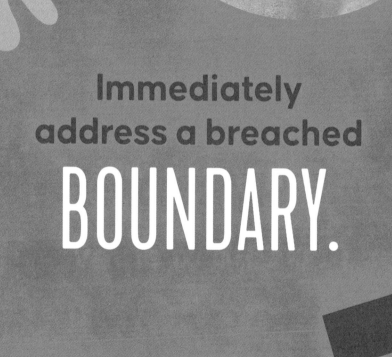

Immediately
address a breached

# BOUNDARY.

There are times when boundaries are breached within the work environment or within professional relationships. Whether the breach is intentional or unintentional, identify and address when a boundary has been breached. This will not only protect you, but it will also create a healthy system of interaction.

> **Identify a time when a boundary was breached and you did not address it.**
>
> **How did the breach make you feel? Identify one way you can communicate when a breach occurs.**

..................................................................................................................................

..................................................................................................................................

..................................................................................................................................

..................................................................................................................................

..................................................................................................................................

..................................................................................................................................

..................................................................................................................................

..................................................................................................................................

..................................................................................................................................

..................................................................................................................................

..................................................................................................................................

..................................................................................................................................

..................................................................................................................................

..................................................................................................................................

# DISENGAGE

from unproductive
conversations.

There are times within the work environment that you may be looped into conversations that are unproductive, be they office gossip or a coworker sharing intimate details about their personal life that you did not ask for. Disengaging from those conversations, or removing yourself from the environment where those conversations are occurring, is an effective way to establish healthy boundaries within the work environment.

**Within your work environment, what are two ways you can avoid unproductive conversations?**

You are

# MORE

than just an
employee.

Leave work at work. The other hats you wear deserve the same amount of time and attention that you give your organization, if not more. Know that you are still a good employee even if you leave work at work.

**What prevents you from detaching from your work identity and tasks?**

**What are two ways you can decompress from the workday in order to be present in other areas of your life?**

Reward yourself
for your hard work
by making time to

# DETACH.

Silence your work notifications. The emails will be there, the questions will be there, and so will the tasks. Silencing your work notifications is a great way to create a healthy work-life balance.

**What stops you from silencing your work notifications?**
**Identify two ways you would benefit from tending to work-related tasks only during work hours.**

# NOTICE

what empties
your cup and
doesn't refill it.

Depending on the components of a task or project you have to complete, there are times when you may feel compelled to work outside of your delegated work hours. Balance your overtime so you are not left feeling exhausted instead of accomplished.

**How has working overtime impacted your life?**
**What is one thing you can do to balance the amount of overtime you work?**

.......................................................................................................................................................

.......................................................................................................................................................

.......................................................................................................................................................

.......................................................................................................................................................

.......................................................................................................................................................

.......................................................................................................................................................

.......................................................................................................................................................

.......................................................................................................................................................

.......................................................................................................................................................

.......................................................................................................................................................

.......................................................................................................................................................

.......................................................................................................................................................

.......................................................................................................................................................

.......................................................................................................................................................

# MINIMIZE

**working
through lunch.**

Sometimes, it is unavoidable—work tasks spill over into lunchtime. When it is avoidable, take your lunch break without incorporating work-related duties. This is time set aside by your organization for you to regroup. Use it.

**What would you need in order to not work through lunch?**
**What are two ways you can meet that need?**

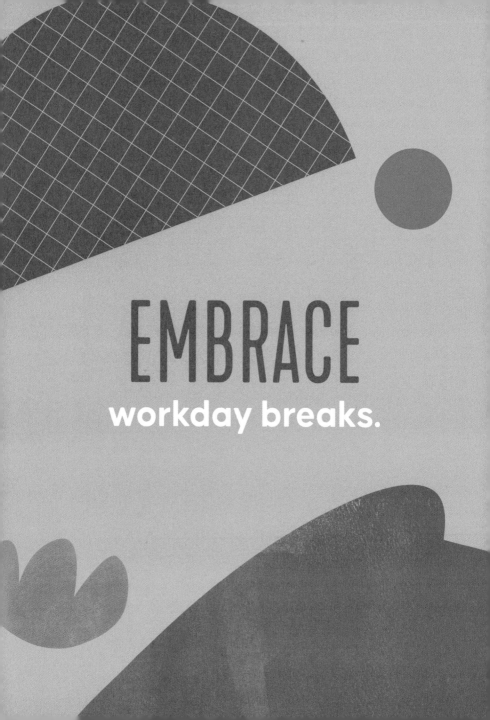

# EMBRACE
**workday breaks.**

Feeling stressed from work-related tasks can impact your ability to be productive. Lunch breaks are sometimes just not enough. When you are feeling overwhelmed or unable to concentrate, step away from the task, take a walk, or engage in a mindfulness activity.

Identify one or two bodily signals that let you know you are overwhelmed.

With your work area in mind, what are two things you can do to recenter yourself?

# Give yourself
## space to
# RECOVER.

You are not performing at your optimal productivity level when you are not feeling well. In addition, you run the potential of making mistakes that could hinder progress or cause you to do additional work to rectify the mistake. You are human, and there will be times that you fall ill. If you have sick leave, use it.

**Are you afraid to use your sick leave? Why?**
**What would make you feel comfortable enough to use your sick leave?**

Take the time
you have

EARNED.

You do not need to be sick, attending a doctor's appointment, or managing a crisis to deserve time off from work. Whether it is taking a vacation or just chilling at home, take the time you have earned. The best way to respect your own boundaries is by honoring your limits and rewarding your efforts.

**When do you feel like you deserve time off from work?**
**Look at your calendar. Identify and write down one to two days within the month that you can take time off from work.**

The task can
# WAIT.

If you are on sick leave or paid time off, do not respond to work communications. Receiving work-related questions or requests while you are taking time away from work is a significant boundary violation. Even if it is an easy fix, the task can wait until you return to work.

**How do you normally respond when you receive work-related questions or requests on your days off?**

**What is one way that you can implement or improve your boundaries on your days off from work?**

..................................................................................................................

..................................................................................................................

..................................................................................................................

..................................................................................................................

..................................................................................................................

..................................................................................................................

..................................................................................................................

..................................................................................................................

..................................................................................................................

..................................................................................................................

..................................................................................................................

..................................................................................................................

..................................................................................................................

..................................................................................................................

# COMMUNICATE
**realistic expectations and timelines.**

There may be times when unrealistic expectations or timelines may be applied to a task. One way to honor your boundaries is by communicating an effective timeline for a task to be completed. This way, you are not willingly subjecting yourself to stress that could have been avoided.

Identify a time that you subjected yourself to meeting an unrealistic deadline. How did you feel?

How can you prevent that from reoccurring?

# EXPRESS
**your thoughts
and ideas.**

Not expressing your thoughts and ideas within professional environments can impair how productive you are within the environment. Sitting on those thoughts can be the result of not feeling safe or not feeling confident in the idea.

**How do you feel when you have a thought or an idea that you do not express?**

**What type of environment makes you feel comfortable enough to express your thoughts and ideas?**

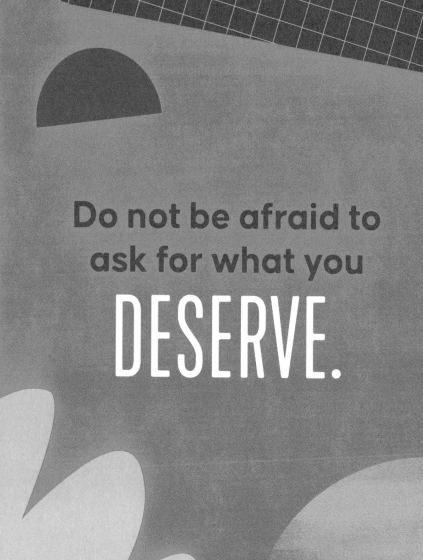

Do not be afraid to ask for what you

DESERVE.

You deserve to be acknowledged and compensated for what you are worth. You do not have to accept what is available because it is the only thing that is being offered.

At your current organization, are you receiving what you are worth?
If not, what made you accept the offer?
What would it take for you to renegotiate the offer?

# ACCEPTING

disrespect is not a part
of the job description.

Identify and communicate how you would like to be addressed. You spend a majority of your time at work, and you have a right to exist comfortably within that environment.

**What organizational behaviors make you feel disrespected, uncomfortable, or unwelcome?**

**What is one way you can address this behavior?**

Know when it
is time to

MOVE ON.

Some environments are just not the right environments for you. Unhealthy environments have a way of changing you before changing themselves. Instead of subjecting yourself to misery, know when it is time to move on.

**What within the work environment makes it intolerable?**
**What will it take for you to permanently separate from it?**

# Tell others what you
# NEED.

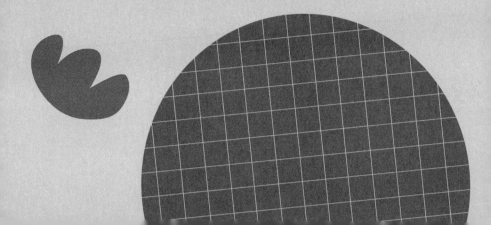

You deserve to feel safe in your relationships. A part of making sure that you are safe and remain safe is by letting others know what your needs are and how you expect those needs to be met. This is a way to proactively set boundaries within all your relationships.

**Identify what makes you feel safe in relationships. How can you communicate that to others?**

.......................................................................................................................................

.......................................................................................................................................

.......................................................................................................................................

.......................................................................................................................................

.......................................................................................................................................

.......................................................................................................................................

.......................................................................................................................................

.......................................................................................................................................

.......................................................................................................................................

.......................................................................................................................................

.......................................................................................................................................

.......................................................................................................................................

.......................................................................................................................................

.......................................................................................................................................

.......................................................................................................................................

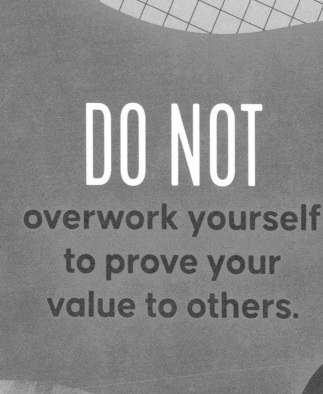

# DO NOT
## overwork yourself to prove your value to others.

---

Giving more than you are receiving can lead to burnout fairly quickly, and being undervalued only expedites that process.

**What areas of your life are you giving more than you are receiving? Identify two ways you can establish a balance between the two.**

Do not allow
yourself to
# SETTLE.

Sometimes, if what you want seems inaccessible then there may be times that you find yourself settling for what's available. You deserve what you want, and you do not have to settle for anything less.

**In what areas of your life have you accepted what was available even though it wasn't what you really wanted?**

# KNOW
## when to
## get involved.

You do not have to be superhuman for everyone you know, love, or come into contact with. You can protect your peace by knowing when to get involved in situations and what to ignore.

Identify a time when you got involved in a situation that did not require your involvement.
What can you do to not cross that boundary going forward?

........................................................................................................................

........................................................................................................................

........................................................................................................................

........................................................................................................................

........................................................................................................................

........................................................................................................................

........................................................................................................................

........................................................................................................................

........................................................................................................................

........................................................................................................................

........................................................................................................................

........................................................................................................................

........................................................................................................................

........................................................................................................................

........................................................................................................................

........................................................................................................................

# COMMUNICATE

**consequences of
boundary violations.**

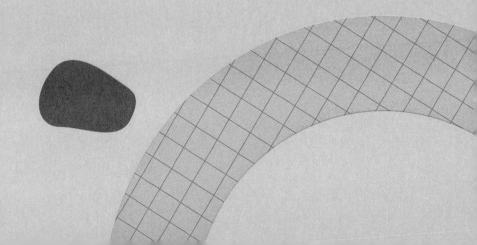

All boundary violations should have a consequence. There is no one-size-fits-all consequence. You have the right to decide how your relationship will look with someone after a boundary violation has occurred.

**What boundary violations do you experience the most and from whom?**

**Identify consequences for those violations.**

.........................................................................................................................

.........................................................................................................................

.........................................................................................................................

.........................................................................................................................

.........................................................................................................................

.........................................................................................................................

.........................................................................................................................

.........................................................................................................................

.........................................................................................................................

.........................................................................................................................

.........................................................................................................................

.........................................................................................................................

.........................................................................................................................

.........................................................................................................................

.........................................................................................................................

.........................................................................................................................

Do not

# SHARE

everything
so quickly.

A well-known way of connecting with someone is to instantly share relatable personal information, but a healthy way of connecting is to know that you do not have to immediately overshare in order to build a relationship. Protecting yourself means protecting your experiences until someone proves they are trustworthy enough to hold that type of information.

**How do you feel after oversharing?**
**How would you know if someone is trustworthy?**

........................................................................................................................................
........................................................................................................................................
........................................................................................................................................
........................................................................................................................................
........................................................................................................................................
........................................................................................................................................
........................................................................................................................................
........................................................................................................................................
........................................................................................................................................
........................................................................................................................................
........................................................................................................................................
........................................................................................................................................
........................................................................................................................................
........................................................................................................................................
........................................................................................................................................

Know that you can
be free and still be

# UNAVAILABLE.

You have the right to be unavailable for whatever you so choose. Be intentional about what you expose yourself to, and always check in with yourself before responding and before saying yes to a request.

**What do you like to do with your free time?**

**What can you do to make sure that your free time remains just for you?**

........................................................................................................................

........................................................................................................................

........................................................................................................................

........................................................................................................................

........................................................................................................................

........................................................................................................................

........................................................................................................................

........................................................................................................................

........................................................................................................................

........................................................................................................................

........................................................................................................................

........................................................................................................................

........................................................................................................................

........................................................................................................................

........................................................................................................................

........................................................................................................................

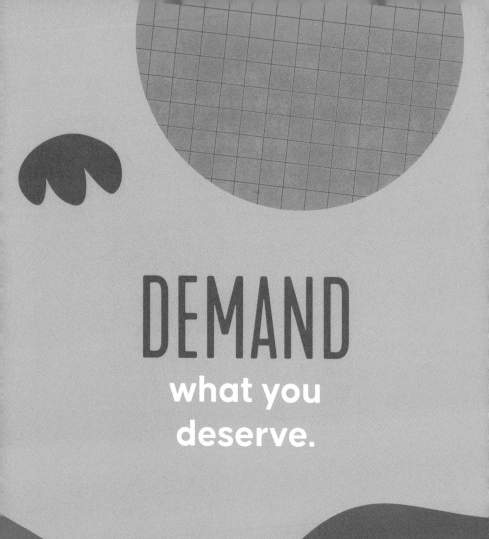

# DEMAND

## what you deserve.

If someone is not capable of delivering what you
deserve, it does not mean you are asking for too much—
it means you are asking for it from the wrong person or place.

**What is stopping you from demanding what you deserve?**
**What would you demand if you didn't have that barrier?**

# MINIMIZING

**what you need will not erase your desire for the need to be met.**

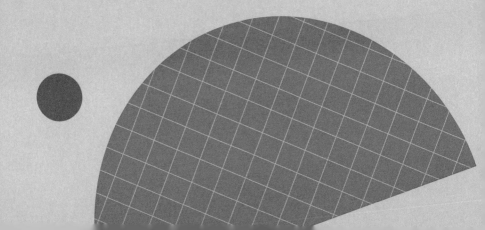

Do not minimize your needs. Your needs will
not look like the needs of someone else.

**What needs have you minimized and why?**
**Identify your top needs and what should be done to meet them.**

.......................................................................................................................

.......................................................................................................................

.......................................................................................................................

.......................................................................................................................

.......................................................................................................................

.......................................................................................................................

.......................................................................................................................

.......................................................................................................................

.......................................................................................................................

.......................................................................................................................

.......................................................................................................................

.......................................................................................................................

.......................................................................................................................

.......................................................................................................................

.......................................................................................................................

.......................................................................................................................

.......................................................................................................................

.......................................................................................................................

# MANAGE

### what you give
### your attention to.

Everything and everyone do not deserve your attention.
Social media, the news, and other stimuli can be both helpful
and harmful. You are violating your boundaries by investing your
time and attention into areas that can be unhealthy for you.

What unhealthy areas or situations have your attention the most?
Identify two ways you can modify what you give your attention to.

Do not make someone else's **URGENCY** your emergency.

You do not have to say yes just because someone asked, and you do not have to respond immediately because someone else is in a rush. You are allowed to process what you want to do and say before giving an answer.

**What happens when you feel rushed to do something or give a response?**

**How can you incorporate pausing before providing an answer?**

Give yourself

# PERMISSION

to say "This no longer works for me."

What you tolerated yesterday can be given a boundary today.
When you are able to identify how you want to be treated and stand by it,
you are less likely to accept being treated outside of that preference.

**How do you want to be treated?**
**What behaviors no longer work for you?**

# TRUST
**your instincts before trusting someone's judgment.**

Making decisions can sometimes be difficult, be they simple or complex. Before accepting someone's opinion, check in with yourself to see if your instincts naturally align.

**What decisions have been the hardest for you to make?**
**What bodily signals let you know if you agree or disagree with something?**

........................................................................................
........................................................................................
........................................................................................
........................................................................................
........................................................................................
........................................................................................
........................................................................................
........................................................................................
........................................................................................
........................................................................................
........................................................................................
........................................................................................
........................................................................................
........................................................................................
........................................................................................
........................................................................................
........................................................................................

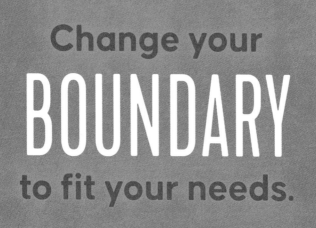

Change your

# BOUNDARY

to fit your needs.

As you evolve, so will your needs. The only time your boundary should change is to adjust to your needs, not the feelings or needs of others.

**Identify a boundary of yours that you need to adjust.**
**What steps can you take to modify that boundary?**

Do not

# NEGOTIATE

your boundary.

Those who are used to having unlimited access to you may not agree with your boundaries. They may push back, and that is okay. Your boundaries are there for a reason; protecting yourself means standing firm on your decision.

**How have you negotiated your boundaries before?**

**How can you communicate your boundaries in a way that doesn't make them optional?**

# Do not
# ACCEPT
## all advice.

There are times where there is a disconnect between someone's intent and their impact even if they mean well. Unsolicited advice can, at times, be helpful, but know that you are not obligated to accept, internalize, or apply any or all advice you may receive.

How do you respond to unsolicited advice?

Develop a phrase you would like to use when you're given unsolicited advice.

# DECLINE

**the invite or
leave the scene.**

One way to respect your own boundaries is by not forcing yourself to stay in environments where you do not feel welcomed. Whether you need to decline an invitation or leave an event early, know that you are not wrong for doing what you need to do to protect yourself.

**What makes you feel unwelcome in social environments?**
**What is the best way that you can distract or protect yourself in unwelcoming environments?**

......................................................................................................
......................................................................................................
......................................................................................................
......................................................................................................
......................................................................................................
......................................................................................................
......................................................................................................
......................................................................................................
......................................................................................................
......................................................................................................
......................................................................................................
......................................................................................................
......................................................................................................
......................................................................................................
......................................................................................................

# STOP

trying to control how others will respond to your boundary.

Your boundaries do not have to be liked by others or easily digestible for them. Some people will have adverse reactions to your boundaries because they will no longer be able to have access to you like they're accustomed to. A part of setting boundaries is knowing that others are entitled to their feelings, but their feelings do not have to influence your boundary.

In what ways have you tried to make sure that others respond well to your boundaries?

What can you do to protect yourself and keep your boundary in place when others have a negative response?

# RESPECT

when a boundary
has been set.

Setting boundaries means that you will also be on the receiving end of a boundary at some point. The respect you would want for your boundary is the same respect you should give to someone else's boundary.

**How do you feel when someone sets a boundary with you? In what ways have you violated someone's boundary?**

# NO MORE
**boundary apologies.**

You do not have to apologize for setting a boundary. Continuously apologizing will lead to you feeling guilty, which could then influence you to withdraw the boundary. You will start to feel confident in setting boundaries when you cease apologizing for them.

**What personal tools or phrases can you use to avoid apologizing for your boundaries?**

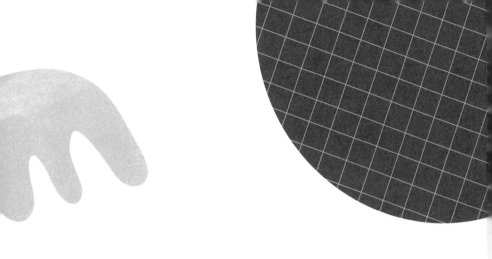

## About the Author

**Asha Gibson** is a licensed professional counselor based in Louisiana. Asha has worked in various areas of the mental health field and is passionate about helping others navigate their individual path to healing.
You can find her on Instagram @SheSpeaksTherapy.